For Peter & Sue,
with eternal thanks
for teaching me
God's Word.

First printed 2008

ISBN 978-1-84625-134-4

British Library Cataloguing in Publication Data available

Published by Day One Publications
Ryelands Road, Leominster, HR6 8NZ
TEL 01568 613 740 FAX 01568 611 473
email—sales@dayone.co.uk
web site—www.dayone.co.uk

Written and illustrated by Donna Drion,
compiled by Kathryn Chedgzoy
and printed by Polskabook, Poland

With thanks to
my husband, Tom,
for his constant love
and encouragement.
This would never have
happened without you!

Stop and look at God's Word

words and pictures by Donna Drion

Book three of a series of three

Have you ever stopped to look at God's Word and thought about how wonderful it is that God has given us a book?

The sun, moon
and stars tell us
about God.

They show us
that God is big
and powerful.

Every day they
remind us that
God is always
everywhere.

Psalm 19

The tiny insects tell us about God; they show us that God cares about everything He has made, even the little things!

But in God's book, the Bible, God speaks to us Himself. He tells us what He is like.

He tells us what we are like, and why we are here.

God tells us what He did a long time ago, and what He will do in the future.

When you read God's book,
remember you are reading the words
of the Person who made the stars.
The Bible tells you how you can come
to know the God who made you.
You can know Him as your Father,
as your Saviour, as your friend.

God is good!

In the beginning, everything was always good. God made everything good.

The first two people were holy and happy.

So—why isn't everything good now?

Things are not good because we are not good. Adam and Eve did the one thing God told them not to. Then they tried to hide from God. They became sinful and unhappy.

It is sin that makes things sad and bad.

We are like Adam and Eve. We don't want to keep God's good laws. We want our own way instead. We all sin.

Do you know what sin is? Sin is doing things God says we must not do and sin is not doing things God says we must do.

Telling lies is sin.

Thinking bad thoughts is sin.

God tells us in His Word that sin

makes Him angry and sad.

God is a Judge.

He promises to punish sin.

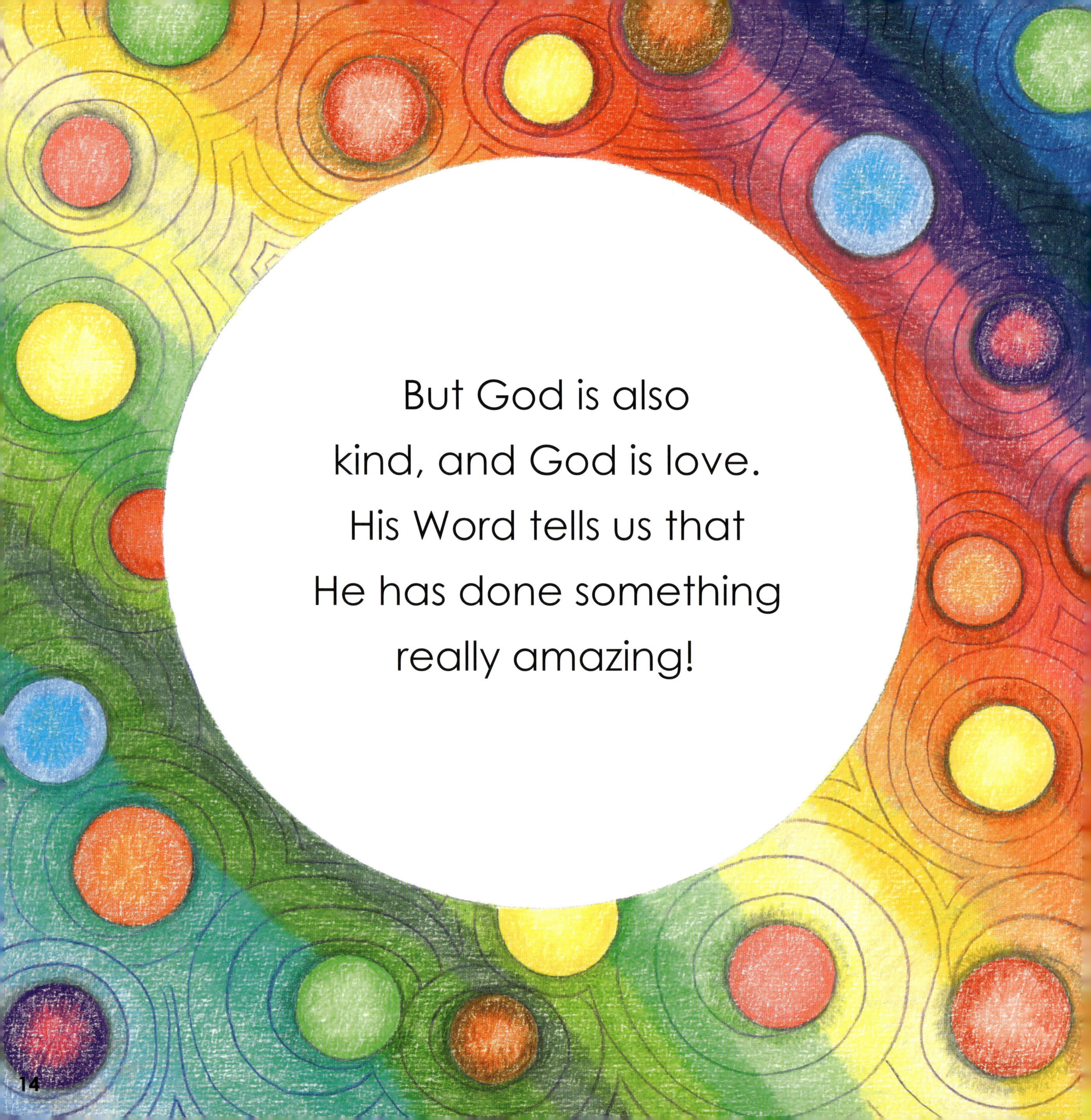

But God is also
kind, and God is love.
His Word tells us that
He has done something
really amazing!

Do you know what it is?

Do you know what God has done for boys and girls just like you?

God sent His Son, Jesus, from heaven to earth. When Jesus was born as a little baby in Bethlehem, the angels were so excited that they burst out of heaven to have a look. They appeared in the sky to some shepherds who were looking after their sheep. The angels said that the Saviour had been born.

Have you ever sung about this at Christmas time?

Jesus was God and man at the same time.
He was good, kind, gentle, holy and true.
Jesus never sinned.

He kept all God's rules all the time.
All the things we couldn't do, Jesus did all the time.
Where we fail, Jesus didn't, not even once.

Jesus was all powerful:
He made the blind see;
He made the deaf hear;
He made the lame jump;
He made the dead rise!

God's Word tells us that Jesus agreed to change places with sinners to save them. He was punished for their sins even though He had never sinned. What difference does that make? That means God will not be angry with them any more. That means God will treat them as if they had done all the good things Jesus did. That means God will be very pleased with them.

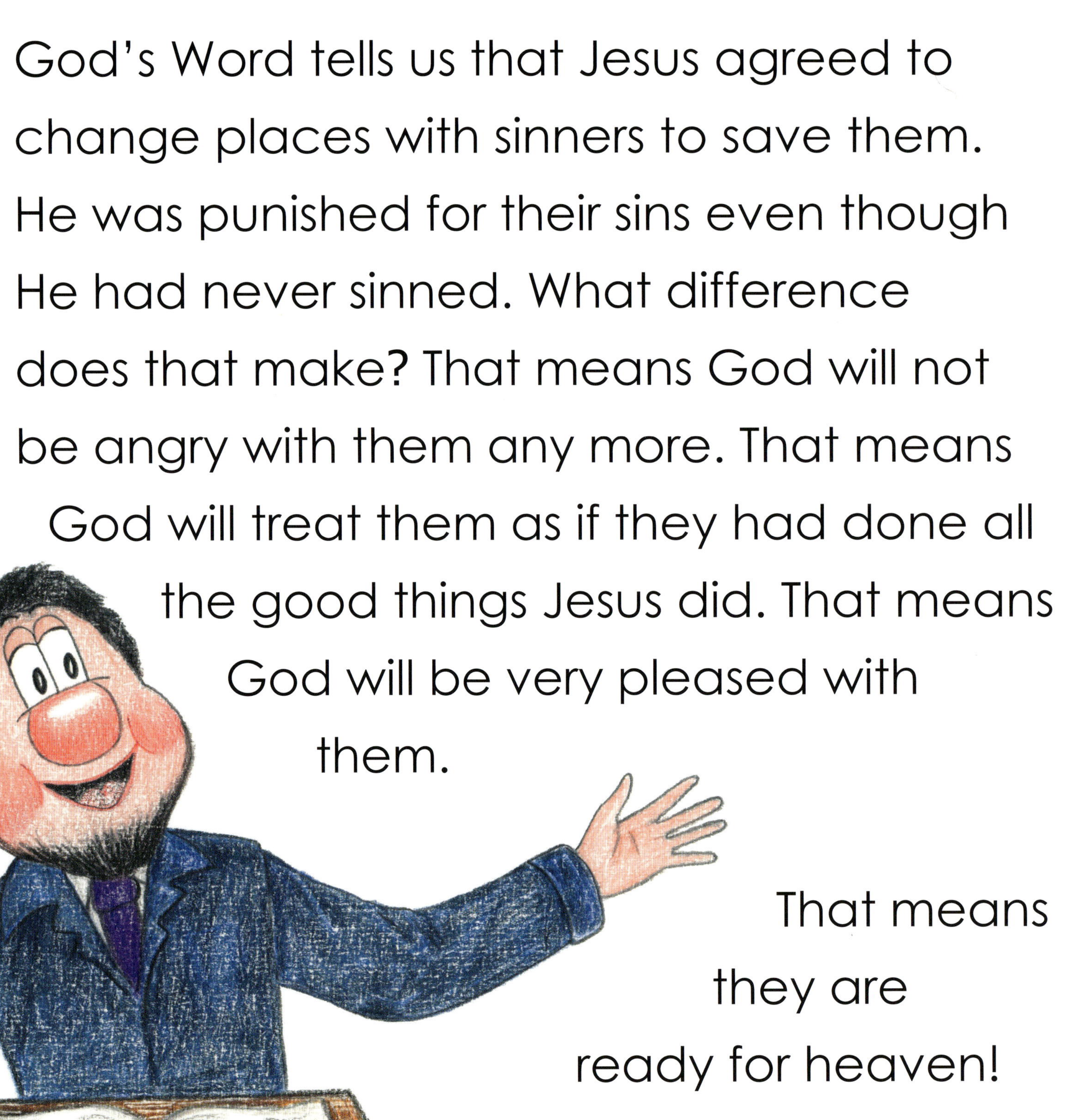

That means they are ready for heaven!

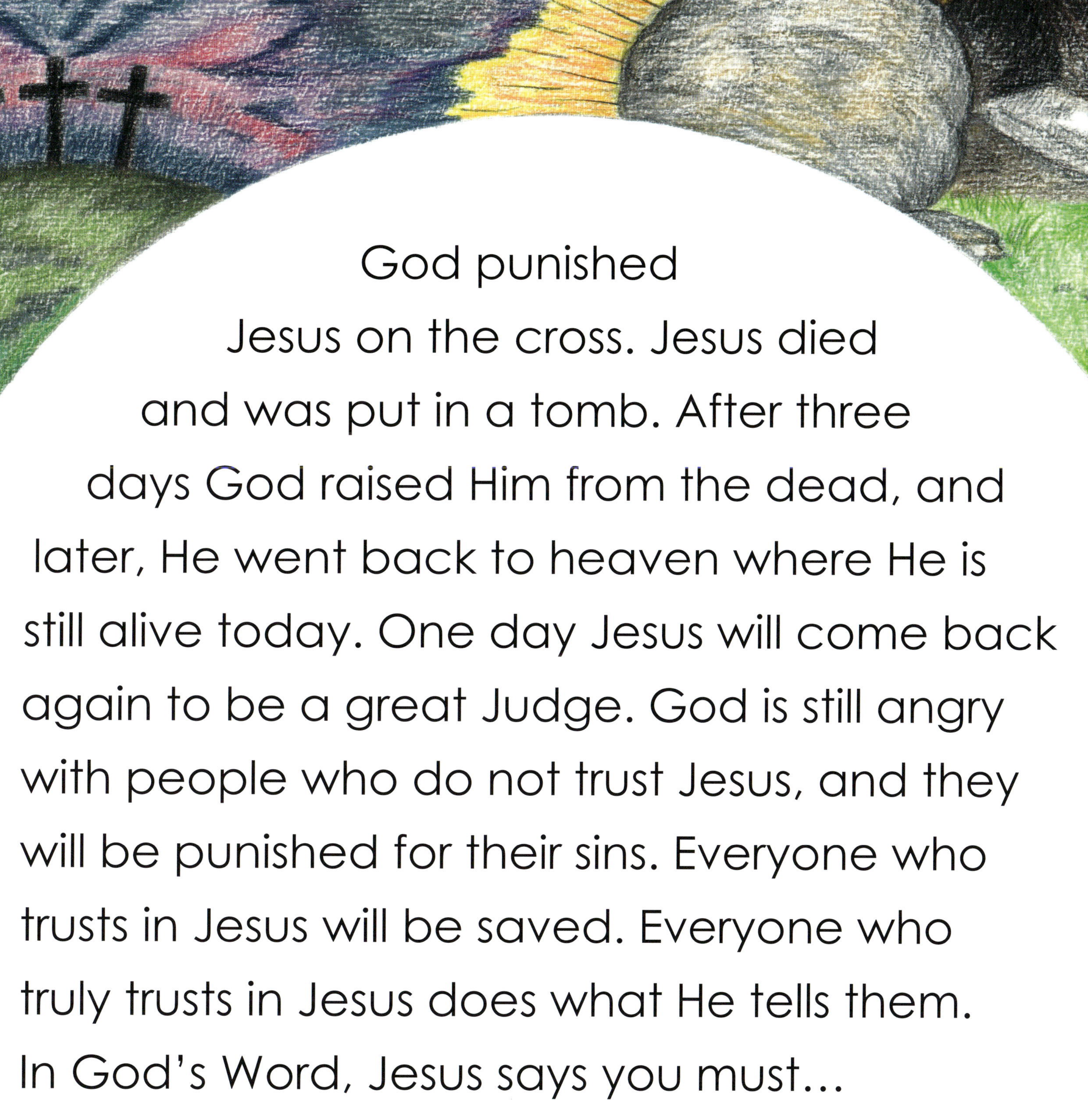

God punished Jesus on the cross. Jesus died and was put in a tomb. After three days God raised Him from the dead, and later, He went back to heaven where He is still alive today. One day Jesus will come back again to be a great Judge. God is still angry with people who do not trust Jesus, and they will be punished for their sins. Everyone who trusts in Jesus will be saved. Everyone who truly trusts in Jesus does what He tells them. In God's Word, Jesus says you must...

Own up to God and tell Him what you've done.

Pray and ask God to forgive you.

Own up to other people. Put right what you can. Ask God to help you stop sinning.

Because Jesus died for sinners, everyone who trusts in Him is forgiven.

So next time you

look at God's Word,

Stop and remember that
it was God who gave it,
and who came down from
heaven to be the Saviour.

It doesn't matter who you are
or where you are, if you ask Him,
He will be your Saviour, too.

Q) Where do we learn how to love and obey God?

A) In the Bible only.

Q) Who wrote the Bible?

A) Holy men who were taught by the Holy Spirit.

Q) What is sin?

A) Sin is either neglecting to do what God requires or doing what God forbids.

Q) Can anyone go to heaven with a sinful nature?

A) No, our hearts must be changed before we can be fit for heaven.

Q) Who can change a sinner's heart?

A) The Holy Spirit alone.